Spiritual Healing

Hands-On Healing
Conjuring
Correction of pelvic obliquity

© 2018 – Stefan J. Schill. All rights reserved
Herstellung und Verlag: BoD – Books on Demand, Norderstedt
ISBN: 9783746064567

Content:

Part I

Spiritual Healing Instruction

Since March 2004 it is legal to practise spiritual healing in Germany, without being a certified natural health professional. This is an information only for example.

Spiritual Healing is completely legally in many countries. Please, find out about how the law situation is in your country. You get more information about it in your city hall or the city administration.

These lessons will help you to become a spiritual healer, who will support people to overcome their diseases.

Please note:

This text addresses male and female healers alike, although this is not explicitly mentioned to keep this text easily readable.

The training is divided in different parts.

This is, what you will learn:

- Hands-on healing
- Chakra compensation
- Distant treatments
- Conjuring
- Mental treatments
- Correction of pelvic obliquity
- Legal suggestions
- Financial tips
- Code of conduct
- Behaviour towards persons seeking help
- Tips for your own office and your own website

The course is divided in 3 parts. In between these parts, you can already work in your own office to gather experience. Of course you can address me during the time of the instruction and after for at least 2 more years.

At a first glance this seems to be a lot and maybe even too much, but trust me. Everyday experiences show, that the work of a healer is much more extensive. These are just the basics.

An everyday question is: "What is spiritual healing?" The terms "spiritual healing" or "spiritual healer" are quite common, but there are no ghosts or the brain itself involved! "Spiritual healing" is rather "healing through God" or (if you prefer) through a higher instance. This is how the following terms should be understood.

Probably everyone already heard about "wise" women or men, who are able to use incantations to charm away warts and shingles. Again and again there are reports about allegedly faith healers, who have conjured away cancer, HIV, paralysis and other diseases.

Well...be honest...you cannot believe that, can you? Right! Usually it cannot happen that fast, but it is possible to ease or even to heal a disease in several sessions using hands-on healing, reciting prayers or "conjuring". When accepting this form of help, you can also accept, that these treatments will even work without personal contact between patient and healer.

Hard to imagine? This is the usual reaction. Most of the times it happens like this: The doctor says: "I cannot do anything for you anymore. Try... who "conjures" warts, shingles and other diseases..." When a healer treats the patients, they often recover after many years of suffering.

Of course - and needless to say - the treatment of a healer cannot replace a doctor's visit! Every reliable healer will ask his patients, if they are under medical treatment. Remember, that a healer cannot and must not make a diagnosis (unless the healer is a doctor or a natural health professional). Within the meaning of the law the treatment of a healer is not a medical or a naturopathic treatment, because the healer treats the person, who is ill and not the disease itself. It is not a decision between "spiritual healing" or "traditional medicine", rather "medicine" **and** "spiritual healing". If there are acute cases, accidents, and undefined health problems, then a doctor has to be involved first. "Spiritual healing" can help patients with chronic diseases or "beyond treatment". (Someone who suffers from back pain would not only just go to a massage or a physiotherapist either.)

Just imagine a patient with pain in his chest for several days. The healer treats him; the patient feels much better, but dies two hours later because of a heart attack. A correct diagnosis and the right medical treatment in time probably would have saved him.

Another possible case: A very athletic patient has pain in his arm. The healer treats him for several months until it gets a little bit better. During a medical examination, due to other reasons, the doctors discover bone cancer in this arm. If the diagnosis and the medical treatment were made in time, then the disease would have been cured faster and the patient probably healthy again. The cooperation between a doctor and a healer would have been much more effective.

Conclusion:

No reliable healer would advise a patient against going to a doctor and most of them only treat patients, when there is a diagnosis made by a doctor. This is no charlatanry (as some critics assume) to rip ill people off, but an additional treatment, which efficiency was even proven in scientific controlled double-blind trials!

Most healers do not "give" something from themselves! They rather see themselves just as a transmitter between a higher (divine, universal or life) power and the suffering human being. The work of a healer is very much the same work, the clericals have always done (when they followed their clerical duties and brought salvation): Bring God's help and power to the people. Many healers like to think of themselves as chaplains, who care for a healthy soul which cures the body.

Healing is also listening. Many persons seeking help have already been to many doctor's offices and hospitals, until they finally go to a healer. Usually a healer is the last and final attempt just before resignation. Everything else has already been done: x-rays, blood exam, spinal fluid, or even tissue samples have been extracted and other – often painful – examinations have been made. Often with no results or the doctors could not do anything for the patient anymore.

Always listen to the medical records first. You will get important information about the person. The person seeking help can be impatient or rather submissive. There are people who fight for their health and others who already have given up.

The most important question of those, who seek help is always: "Can you help me?" And your answer should be: "I will try." As a healer you can promise to give your best, but you must not promise cure! You cannot know the progress of the disease or how much time is left in the plan of life of the person seeking help. Doctors and natural health professionals cannot promise cure and neither can we.

Hands-on Healing

Hands-on healing is probably one of the oldest healing methods. Each mother uses it intuitively, when her child is ill or has an injury.

There is also a reference in the bible, when Jesus uses hands-on healing to cure ill people. But there is even more, because he also called his disciples to do the same. Matthew 10.8: "Heal the sick, raise the dead, cleanse those who have leprosy, drive out demons. Freely you have received; freely give."

A free treatment was possible in times, when Jesus lived. The healer was a guest for several days and the community gave him food. The times have changed. There are still many healers, who work for free because they have a job to earn money. They usually like to think of their ability as a gift of God. Sometimes a healer discovers his abilities after health problems, an accident, a coma, or other experiences close to death. Some healers "inherit" the ability from an ancestor. Usually these people help other people for free. Those who decided to work full-time as a healer do not need to have a bad conscience though, when they charge money. We will come back to that later.

Which diseases can be treated with spiritual healing?

Basically everyone and every disease can be treated! There are no sufferings, which cannot be treated in a healing session - if it is only easing the pain or helping to die. There are patients though, who do not react to a treatment.

Children of every age (and babies as well) react very well to a treatment. The reasons for the treatment do not matter. It could be neurodermatitis, asthma, rheumatic diseases, or just teething troubles of babies. It is always worth a try. The treatment of children or animals is the best proof, that you do not have to believe in spiritual healing to make it work. You cannot cure children, animals, and plants with the help of their "belief".

For many cancer patients (but also other patients with chronic or often fatal diseases) a healer is their last hope – often with good reason. When the medical conditions get better after a few treatments, or at least chemotherapy or radiotherapy cause less problems, or operation wounds heal "surprisingly fast and without problems" (original quote of a doctor), even the greatest critic has to admit the positive effects of the work of a healer.

In the meantime there are already many doctors, who think:

"If it helps the patient - then why not?"

I have to admit though, that there are some diseases which do not react to spiritual help. Those are the diseases, which destroy organs. For example someone, who suffers from asthma, may find help through a healer, but if there is already a pulmonary emphysema (which destroys a lot of alveoles), then probably no healer can help in "healing" these destroyed alveoles. If a patient has multiple sclerosis, which destroys the myelin of the nerve fibres, no healer will probably be able to help him either. It is still worth a try though, because I have already heard about healers, who were successful at treating MS.

Definition of some Terms

The Aura

The **aura** or **the subtle body** of a living being is according to different doctrines a charisma. Psychic people or human beings, who are sensitive in other ways (so called „synaesthetic") see this charisma in coloured clouds or light coronas around the body. The aura is composed of multiple layers, which have a strong connection to the chakras of the human being. It is quite common to define the aura in seven layers, which correspond to the seven main chakras. There are other layer concepts, because there are also doctrines, which assume more than seven main chakras.

The Chakras

A **chakra** (meaning: wheel, disk, circle) is a subtle energy centre between the material body and the subtle body or the astral body of the living being, according to traditional south Asian concepts of the Tantric Hinduism, the Tantric Buddhistic vajrayana, and the yoga as well to some derived modern European and north American doctrines. The chakras are connected through subtle energy channels. Old Indian and Tibetan texts refer to 72.000 up to 350.000 energy channels in a body. Similar views with another terminology are represented in the Traditional Chinese Medicine (TCM).

Seven chakras are the vital energy centres. They are located in line with the spine and are connected through the flow of the energy (called sushumna or haraline). Through this channel also rises the kundalini power. The number and the localisation of the chakras vary in different doctrines. There are also energy centres outside the human body. Most of them are along the sushumna between heaven and earth.

Chakras and their

Connection to Body and Psyche

The 1st chakra, the root chakra/basis chakra (your foundation):

Relation to the body	Everything solid like the spine, bones, teeth, nails; anus, rectum, colon, intestines, prostate, blood and cellular structure.

Besides the relation to the body, the themes work and money, food and control, existential fears, suspicion, discontent, and personal safety can be added.

Someone who has always trouble with his teeth, has also an unstable 1st chakra and problems with the themes work and money or another key point as well.

The following aspects belong to a stable foundation:

- Safety
- Comfort
- Work
- Order
- Routine
- Nurture (mental and spiritual)
- Sincerity
- Responsibility
- Health

The 2nd chakra, the sacral chakra (your vitality):

Relation to the body	Pelvic area, reproductive organs, kidneys, bladder; everything fluid like blood, lymph, digestive juices, sperm.

Besides the relation to the body, the themes relationships and sexuality, dealing with feelings and your own body, the ability to enjoy and to celebrate, caring for oneself and looking after your appearance, accepting good and getting spoiled and bringing beauty into your own life can be added as well.

Many important points. For example someone, who suffers regularly from inflammations of the bladder, has usually also problems with relationships. Besides medical help the person will also need assistance for this theme. One of the other points may be important as well. Sometimes it is not just one point but many of them and all of them are detectable.

The following aspects belong to vitality:

- Comfort
- Joy
- Romance
- Beauty
- Passion
- Sensuality
- Affection
- Sexuality
- Indulgence
- Desire

Relation to the body	Lower back, abdominal cavity, digestive system, stomach, liver, spleen, gall bladder, autonomic nervous system.

Other themes of this chakra are: the ability to say "no", general fears like phobias, being afraid to speak out, fear of persons of authority, also the feeling of your own safety, knowledge of your own needs (physical and mental), the ability to draw boundaries without exploding, to care for yourself.

A main theme is of course the phobias, but there are also smaller aspects: the well-known disability to say no can have many negative results. Addiction (in many ways) is another special theme of this chakra.

The following aspects belong to personal sovereignty:

- Draw boundaries
- Concentration
- Authority
- Discipline
- Courage
- Believe
- Peace
- Autonomy
- Integrity
- Determination

The 4th chakra, the heart chakra (your heart):

Relation to the body	Heart, upper back with chest and chest cavity, lower lung, blood and blood circulation, skin.

Someone who is easily offended or who does not talk to others for several weeks, as well as the well-known helper syndrome, are hints for an imbalanced heart chakra. Those people often do not like themselves (shows in different ways).

The themes are love, empathy, being fond of yourself, the ability to forgive, as well as happiness, or generosity.

The heart chakra stands for:

- Empathy
- Generosity
- Forgiveness
- Care
- Acceptance
- Affection
- Patience
- Laughing

The 5th chakra, the throat chakra (your self-expression):

Relation to the body	Throat, neck, jaw, ears, vocal cord (voice), trachea, bronchia, upper lung, gullet, arms.

Hints for an imbalanced throat chakra are people, who talk constantly and do not give others a chance to speak. The opposite is also an indication. These people say nothing and they cannot talk about their feelings and needs, although they are often able to talk, when they are engaged in business. Other indications are angry outbursts, insulting other people, or talking someone into guilt feelings. Remarkable are also the whishy-washy type of persons, who never take a stance and always change their mind for the sake of piece and quiet or someone, who never speaks his mind, without hurting others or even badmouths other people.

That looks like a lot, but it is not difficult to recognise. A friend of mine had unexplainable pain in her arm for a lengthy period of time. Nothing really seemed to help and the doctors had no ideas anymore. She realised, that there has to be something unspoken, because she is usually a very positive communicative person. Indeed there was a situation at work, which she talked to her employer about, and then the pain lessened and disappeared.

Other themes are laughter, sincerity, telepathy. The connection to other people often shows in the same thoughts, which the other one articulates, or thinking about someone, who calls at that minute.

These themes stand for harmonic self-expression:

- •Speaking
- •Truth
- •Laughing
- •Listening
- •Creativity
- •Telepathy
- •Affinity

The 6th chakra, the third eye chakra (your personal vision):

Relation to the body	Face, eyes, ears, nose, sinuses, cerebellum, central nervous system.

One problem can be a distorted self-view. If someone is for example an artist or a painter, but this person cannot view oneself as an artist or a painter. An exaggerated "intellectualism" often shows, that someone is not open to human and spiritual experiences. Often these people are always in search of something, which is understandable, because they are missing an important aspect in their life. In relation to the body there are often problems with the sinuses or a reoccurring conjunctivitis or something like that.

These people dream easily, they have daydreams and a good imagination. These are signs for an alert mind. They love to solve problems and are able to see things from the perspective of other people and situations. Other indications for an open third eye chakra are the ability to see behind the outward appearance, watching out for details, and an optimistic attitude to life. And of course the divination, which has a lot to do with this chakra.

To the inner vision belong:

- Perception
- Ability to discriminate
- Dreams
- Memories
- Daydreams
- Divination
- Thinking
- Reason
- Perspective
- Ingenuity

The 7th chakra, the crown chakra (your personal crown):

Relation to the body	cerebrum

A strong theme is the memories of the soul. Indications are for example the feelings of déjà vu or feeling a strong connection to someone, although you only just met him. The so called "midlife crisis" can be an indication for the sudden opening of the crown chakra, because the person now has enough safety in the lower chakras to deal with greater themes.

The crown chakra is the connection to "the big picture", the universe and the plan of the soul. Now you "know" that things are true, without really understanding why. You do not worry anymore and you understand that all experiences make sense regardless of how painful they can be. You trust your inner guidance.

A few of the main themes of the crown chakra:

- Belief
- Memories of the soul
- Follow your own way
- Prayer and meditation
- Thankfulness

Maybe you understand, why I am so excited about this theme. It is also possible to assign colours and healing stones to the chakras. The colours are indicated through the colours of the headlines.

In a lot of times some chakras work together. The root chakra is often connected to the solar plexus chakra, and the sacral chakra to the heart chakra. In that case both chakras show blockades.

Access to practical Experiences

First Exercises

Now let us turn towards the actual hands-on healing

Like in every real healing system (which does not only treat the symptoms) the treatment is based on the opening to God's energy. The healer does not give his own life energy, but functions as a channel for God's energy. Always be aware, that in every session you are a servant of God and his pure energy of love. Of course it is very helpful (for your patient and for you), if you load yourself with life energy before you start the treatment. The treatment will not work well, if the healer is tired and sick looking. Would you trust a doctor, who looks like death himself?

Use the following rituals to load yourself with energy:

1st exercise:

Stand upright in a room (or in the morning after getting out of bed in the open country). Position your feet on shoulder width. Your feet should be under your shoulders. Raise your hands slowly with your palms facing up to the heaven and breathe in deeply, while you move your stretched arms from bottom to the top. After breathing in, you hold your breath for about 2 seconds. Then you let your palms facing to the ground. Lower your arms and hands slowly and breathe out. Then you wait again for about 2 seconds. Then you start all over again!

This is important: Always breathe in through your nose and breathe out through your mouth. Always remember, that you breathe in pure life energy and you breathe out everything, which is negative. Imagine, that you breathe in pure life energy through your crown chakra, which is the highest point on your head. When you breathe out, the negative energy will leave your body through your feet or the basis chakra. After 5 to 10 minutes you have loaded yourself with life energy, which will be enough for the whole day or several treatments.

You have to find out on your own, how many times you have to repeat this exercise. If you have done for example three treatments, and after the third session you feel tired or weak, then you should already repeat this exercise after the second treatment.

It works best, when you use the so called "abdominal breathing": Push your belly to the front when you breathe out. This brings your midriff to the bottom and makes space for the extending lung. After you have done this for several times, you might feel a tingling in your back and shoulders. This is a signal for being filled to the maximum.

2nd exercise:

Stand still in a room or in the open country. Concentrate to breathe in light or energy through your crown chakra, and breathe out through your sacral or basis chakra. Hold onto your underarms, while doing this exercise.

Now feel the power floating from the crown chakra through your heart into your hands – then back through your heart and again into your hands and so on. After some time you will begin to "spin" slightly: The energy will flow like a heavy fluid from your heart into your hands and back. Lightly at first, getting heavier and heavier, the more energy is loaded.

It works best, when you have a stable footing. Then the powerful energy cannot throw you off balance.

After some time (not longer than 5-10 minutes) you will feel, that it is enough. Then you will be filled to the maximum.

Some exercises to get used to energy work

Hold your hands in front of your body and the palms facing each other. Then hold the hands at a body width distance. Move the hands very slowly together again. If you look in between your hands, you might see a slight aura at the palms which looks like flickering heat. Maybe you cannot see it at the first time. Perhaps your eyes need some time to recognise the aura.

Move the hands very slowly together. Just before your palms touch, you will feel a slight resistance like a soap bubble in between your hands. Maybe you cannot feel it at the first time, but after a few days practising you will feel the energy.

When you have learnt to see the aura in between your hands, then you might also see the aura around your head (or around the head of your partner or your patients): Stand or sit at a distance of around 2-3 meters away from your partner and watch his head in front of a light background. Around the head you can see a slight "flickering", when it is normal daylight (cloudy). It needs a bit of practice, but most people can see this flickering at least after three days. With a bit of additional practice, you will see colours in this aura as well.

When you have done these exercises, you should load yourself with energy in the way, which was already described. After that you should do these energy exercises again. You will feel the energy much better.

The Treatment

A word of advice first...

Practice a treatment, before you start treating a patient:

Take a chair and place a teddy, or a doll on it, or just imagine a client sitting on that chair. Then start the treatment. At first you might feel a bit stupid, but those exercises will help you with your confidence. No client will trust a healer, who has to look up every move in his papers, while talking to himself: "What else should I do?"

Place the patient on a chair or a stool. It is important to be able to touch the spine completely.

Why a stool or a chair and (sometimes) no couch?

If the patient is lying on a couch, you have to move a lot around to treat him. I have already measured it: You need at least 12 steps to go around a treatment couch and only 5-6 steps to go around a chair. A couch also needs a lot more space, than a chair. And if you cannot work in your treatment room - for whatever reasons - you can always find a chair. Furthermore, there a many patients, who do not like to lay on a treatment couch, because they feel like they are at the mercy of the healer. Sitting on a chair is much better. They get the feeling, they are actively involved in the treatment and can get up anytime they want. If your treatment room is big enough for a couch, then use it. But only use it, when it is best for the treatment and the patient as well. Talk to him first and you will find out, what will be the best way to treat him. Always tell your patient, that you will touch him (or her) on the head, at the shoulders, on the back, on affected parts, and other areas on the body. Maybe you will get advice during the treatment through your guardian angel, spiritual guide, or another higher being to touch other parts of the body to lead energy over there.

Important:

Maybe you have to touch your client on the breast or the genital area. Especially, if you are a male healer with a female patient, this can easily be seen as sexual harassment. If you have to touch your patient there, then first place the hand of the patient there and then your own hand on top. Tell her, what you are going to do to avoid misunderstandings.
Furthermore, the clients should always tell immediately, if they feel unwell (dizziness, breathing troubles etc.). Some clients relax that much during a treatment, that their chest collapses. This can lead to shortness of breath, precordial anxiety etc. Remember, that the client should always sit up straight. A bit of relaxing is good, but it should not become a total shut down.

Sometimes you can get the advice to lay your hands on body parts, which do not seem to have a connection with the actual disease. When you treat, for example problems with the heart, you get the advice to touch the feet, or you treat bilious complaints and you feel you have to touch the temples. Do not become unsure! Follow your intuition! This is your best teacher and advisor!

At first 2-3 minutes per position are right to begin with!

Getting started...

Maybe you feel, you have to pray before beginning a treatment. If that is the case, then do it!

For example:

"Lord, I beg you, let me be your tool, to lead your power in your name to this human being."

When you lay your hands on the patient, just remember, that God's energy flows through your hands into the patient. You can intensify the flow of the energy, when you concentrate on the energy coming in through your crown chakra, while breathing in and flowing through your hands into the patient, while you breathe out. You do not have to will or force something. Everything happens on its own. Trust God's guidance.

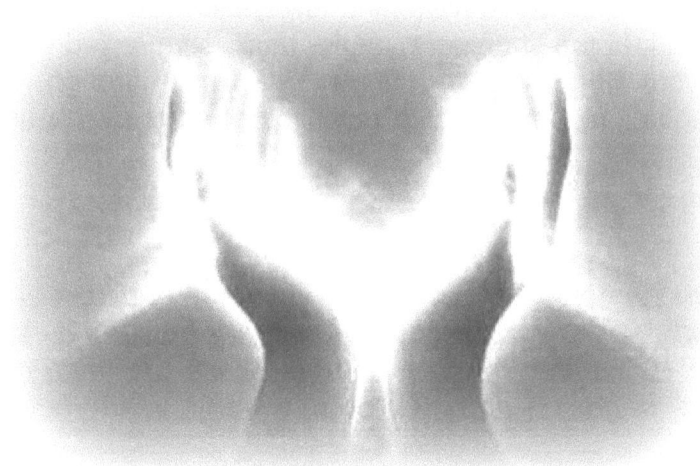

Chakra Compensation

Every treatment begins with a chakra compensation. I learnt this from a reiki teacher, although this form of treatment has nothing to do with reiki.

Each human being has 7 "Gates of Energy", called chakras. Through these chakras flows the energy of life into the human being:

These are the main chakras (from top to bottom):
1. Crown chakra (on top of the head)
2. Forehead chakra (the so called third eye)
3. Neck or throat chakra
4. Heart chakra
5. Solar plexus chakra (over the navel)
6. Sacral chakra (lower belly)
7. Root chakra (between anus and genitals)
The traditional counting of the chakras starts usually at the bottom.

Apart from these main chakras, there are many "sub chakras" like for example the hand chakras, through which the life energy flows into the patient.

The chakra compensation will balance differences in the energy potential of the chakras. After that, all chakras will receive the same amount of energy.

It works best, when the patient is lying either on the floor or on a treatment couch. The healer stands (or sits) on the side of the laying patient, and holds one hand over the crown chakra and the other hand over the root chakra. If it is the left or the right hand, which is over the crown chakra, depends on your position. Are you standing on the left side of the patient, then your right hand is over the crown chakra. But if you are standing on the right side of the patient, then it is the left hand which is over the crown chakra. You do not have to lay your hands down on the chakra. Keep them a few centimetres above. Then try to feel the energy of both chakras. Usually you feel more energy on the crown chakra. In the next step you try to collect energy from the crown chakra with your hand, in time with your breathing (it could be called "breathing into the hand"). Then you give this energy through your other hand to the root chakra. Do this for several breathes of air (about 5-10 breathes). After that, you change the position of the hands. Now one hand is over the forehead chakra (third eye) and the other hand over the sacral chakra (lower belly). The compensation works in the same way, as already described. Then one hand is placed over the throat chakra and the other hand over the solar plexus chakra (over the navel) to do another compensation. Then you place again one hand over the crown chakra and the other hand over the heart chakra for the next compensation.

The chakra compensation always works with 2 chakras:

Crown and root chakra
Forehead and sacral chakra
Throat and solar plexus chakra
Crown and heart chakra

This treatment should be made during the first 2-3 sessions with the patient. You can omit them in later sessions.

Now the actual treatment can start, but first you can use scanning, which has already been used in ancient times: Hold your hands a few centimetres away from the body of the patient. Now move your hands along the body, through the aura, and try to feel something. Whatever it is, every unusual feeling is important. Maybe you feel differences on some parts. This can be heat or cold. Maybe it is a tingling or a shivering of your hand. It does not matter, what it is: Remember this region, when you start the treatment. It can be a harmless inflammation, or a dangerous tumour, maybe the gall bladder was removed, or the spleen. It can be troubles from an operation scar, which turned already into a chronic pain or a cancer, which has not yet been diagnosed. No matter what: Pay special attention to that region during the treatment! Make a mental note of that point and treat that region special. Remember, that you are not allowed to tell your patient about your discovery (unless you are a natural health professional or a doctor), because this could be interpreted as a "diagnosis", which healers are not allowed to make. Just try to give your patient a hint. If there is for example a patient, who wants to be treated because of haemorrhoids, then you can tell him: "I have just read in a magazine, that haemorrhoids may be caused by a dysfunctional bile drainage. Maybe you should go to a doctor to get that checked." This would be a general hint to an article in a magazine, which is legal. Be careful though, that you do not scare your patient unnecessarily. A hint of a possible tumour can cause panic and depression, which then weakens the power of resistance and even causes the outbreak of the tumour!

Scanning

Start with the so called "scanning": Move your hands slowly through the aura of your patient. Watch every detail. If there are problems in the body, then they leave marks in the aura as well. In your first conversation, the patient has probably told you about his problems. Often (but not always) there is also a disorder in the aura around the region of his problems (stomach ache, uterus cancer, migraine etc.). Be very sensitive in that region. In time, you will learn to feel these interfering fields in the aura, without the patient telling them.

No matter, if you felt interfering fields or if the client told you about them: At first you should clean the aura. Therefore you move your hands through the aura to remove disturbing energy. Spread your fingers a little. Then you can "comb" the aura with your fingers. Be very careful in the regions, where you found interfering fields, or where the patient told you about problems.

Then you should get rid of the "combed out" interfering fields. This works best with fire or salt water. I use a burning candle. You can also just imagine a burning fire, in which you burn the negative energy. (Remember though, that a burning candle causes a harmonic atmosphere as well, which will help a healing treatment.) Do not just put the energy "somewhere", because it can be swirled up - like dust - and then cling to your own aura (or the aura of your client, who you just relieved from interfering fields). This would cause an endless cycle of removing and absorbing of negative energy.

Before you start the actual treatment, remember that you are only the channel for the energy!

Hands-on Healing

Always start with laying your hands on the shoulders of the patient for 2-3 minutes. No matter, what the problems are, always begin with the shoulders! The shoulders are very responsive to energy and very sensitive. The patient feels secure, can build trust, and feels, that you will care for him and his problems.

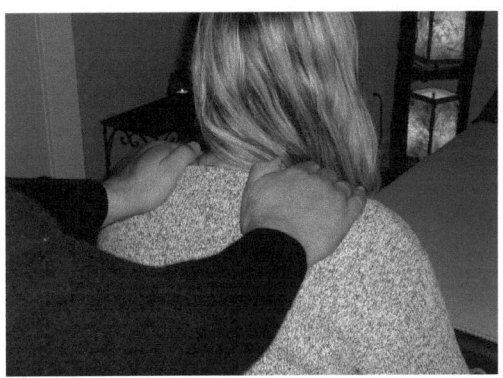

After 2-3 minutes you place your hands on the upper part of the back parallel to the spine.

After another 2-3 minutes you place your hands "one step lower".

Now you can move even deeper, until you reach the waist. This is usually enough, unless there is a disease in the pelvis region (bladder, genitals etc.) or you get a hint from your guardian angel about another part of the body.

If you have to touch your client in the genital area or your female patient on the breast, then first place the hand of the patient there and then your own hand on top.

The energy will be transmitted from you to the hand of the patient and then into the body. If you treat your patient in that way, you can avoid any accusations of sexual harassment.

In the next position, you place your hands on the head of the patient.

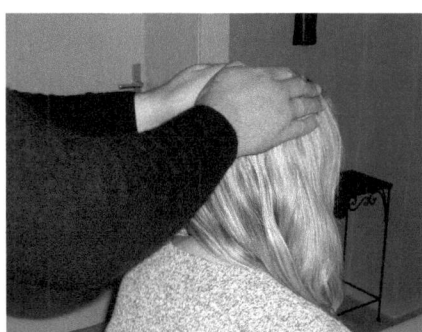

Then you place your hands a little bit more to the sides. The bottom parts of your hands are right above the ears.

When the treatment is over, you can touch your patient twice very lightly at the upper arms. This is the sign, that the treatment is over.

Distant treatment

You can treat your patients also, when they are not physically there. If you do not know your patient personally, then a photo would be helpful. If you know him already and you have met him for example in another treatment, then the distant treatment works without photo. Get in contact, addressing his higher self: "I call the higher self of NN (say the name of the patient). Now I send you the healing energy."

If you need to, then you can hold your hands in the general direction of the addressed patient, but it is not necessary. Just concentrate on the photo of the patient and send him the energy. Perhaps you can see the energy moving towards the recipient through your third eye. Often the energy can be seen as a white or golden whirl. If you cannot see that, then you still need time practising - the time arrives.

After some time - usually 5-10 minutes - you will feel, that the flow of the energy recedes. This is the right moment to stop the distant treatment.

When you do a distant treatment, you are not bound to a certain time. There is no space and time, like we know it, at the place of origin, where this healing energy comes from! When, for example, you promised a patient to do a distant treatment at 21h in the evening for a duration of 15 minutes, then you can also do this treatment at 9h in the morning. Just change the addressing text like this: "I call the higher self of NN (say the name of the patient). The healing energy will get to you this evening starting at 21h in your time zone for a duration of 15 minutes."

It is also possible to initiate multiple distant treatments for different times (for example: "I send you today's energy on every second day in between 18.00 to 18.15"). I do not feel well with this form of "automatic treatment". I prefer being busy with the treatment in that time. But sometimes it cannot be avoided and then this kind of treatment can be used.

Self treatments

Self treatments are possible as well. With a self treatment the body can be cleaned and diseases cured, but it is also good for your own spiritual development. Usually you will feel a tingling or warmth during a self treatment. Sometimes you can see angels or other energy entities. Scents like rose, incense, sandalwood, vanilla, etc. are always signs of present helpers from the spiritual dimension (angels, spiritual helper, etc.).

Place your hands on your belly. One hand with the lower edge on the navel and the other hand above. In that way the complete upper belly is covered. After 2 to 3 minutes the position of the hands will be changed. Then the arms are crossed in front of the chest and the hands placed on the shoulders. The left hand is on the right shoulder and the right hand on the left shoulder.

If your arms get heavy during the first position (hands on the belly lying down), then you can get two cushions and place them left and right under the arms.

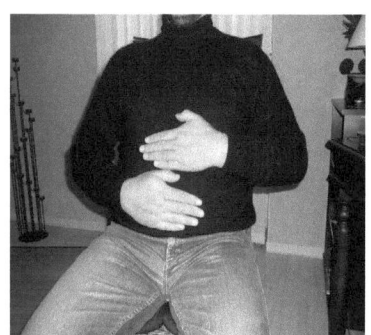

Of course, you can also place your hands on your head, on your ears, or on other parts. These described hand positions are usually working for the most health problems and for spiritual growth.

If you want to treat visible health problems, like for example neurodermititis, open wounds, or something like that, then you should imagine your body in a healthy condition during the self treatment. In case of neurodermititis, the soft healed skin and in case of wounds, the healed body parts.

This kind of visualisation supports of course the healing on other people as well. Therefore you can also use it on other persons.

Part II

Incantations to charm away warts, shingles and other diseases

Conjuring and using incantations are probably the oldest healing arts of the world. In every village, there used to be a witch or a wise woman, who was able to heal diseases through the citation of prayers and sayings.

Probably every human being has this ability as a latent faculty. But of course not everyone is interested to use it or is just not very good at it. That is the same with other things like driving a car or singing. Everyone can do it, but not as well as everybody. According to my experiences as a healer for many years, it is possible to use this ability, when you are really interested in it.

Traditionally the sayings and prayers, which were uttered over a wound, a disease, a wart, etc. were kept secret. Not much has changed though. Because even today not many will give away their own sayings, unless it is for their successor, who usually has to belong to the family. The reason is not relationship, but rather safety, because in former times a lot of people with this ability were suspected to be in league with the devil and were sentenced to the stake. This is the reason, why this art was passed on to relatives, who rather kept quiet and did not go to the officials.

The "scientific thinking" is the reason, why this family tradition will more and more disappear. And all the people, who are interested in this art do not have the possibility to learn these sayings.

Therefore I collected my own sayings and also a few, which were sent to me to publish them for everyone, who is interested. Hopefully, this art will not die out.

How do you use these sayings?

Usually the conjurer holds the hand above the sick area, warts, etc. Then the saying, the prayer, or how you want to call it, is announced three times. After that the "treatment" is finished.

I learnt - and it proved to work - that the treatment has to be repeated three times with a week each inbetween. Do not be surprised, when the wart or the problem disappears already after one or two treatments and the patient does not want to come back. Especially warts and shingles react very quickly to the sayings. Warts for example fall off, dry in, or shrink until they cannot be seen anymore - everything is possible.

But there are other cases as well. Sometimes there does not seem to happen anything at all even after three weeks... Be patient! Sometimes warts, etc. can be persistent. Your patient should wait 2-3 months. In this time most of the sick areas will disappear. If the wart is still there after 3 months, try the sayings again. When that does not work as well, then give your patient the advice to go to another healer.

I also have patients, who go to another healer after 3 months of treatment, because they think the treatment was not successful. Shortly after that, they will be cured. These are powers we cannot influence or understand. We just have to accept them!

Use also hands-on healing during the sayings! This combination often works so well, that the patient is cured after the second session. I tried this combination on a small boy, who came to me because of his warts. After the third treatment the warts were still there. But the mother told me, that the asthma of her son - which she did not tell me, as it already was a permanent element of his life - was suddenly gone. The warts disappeared 3 weeks after the last treatment.

If you want to treat warts and other problems, which should decrease, do the sayings during decreasing moon, that is between full moon and new moon. If you want something to form and to build up, like the healing of wounds and recovery, then you should chose the time of the increasing moon, that is between new moon and full moon.

These are the sayings for different diseases:

Warts, myomas, cysts
What I see, this disappears.
What I touch, this becomes soft.
Wart – go away!

Warts (2)
Speak the following words on
the wart. Your breath should
touch the wart:
Frene, Frene, dorra – go away,
Frene, Frene, dorra – go
away;
In the name of the Father and
the Son and the Holy Spirit.

This has to be repeated three times and, when the three highest names are mentioned, you have to blow on the treated area after each of the names. In a few weeks they just disappear.

–

Warts (3)

The time comes. The time goes. The good things stay here. The bad things go away.

Shingles, facial erysipelas, herpes, cytomegaly, chickenpox, herpes, karposi sarcoma. All "women's disorders"
The Mother of God moved through the land,
she held three roses in the hand,
the 1st was white, the 2nd red, the 3rd was the death.

Shingles (2)

Jerusalem - A tree with roses stands on a dam close to it.
The tree. He does not blossom. He gets no fruits.
You! Rose! Stop to blossom and gets no more fruits.
In the name of the Father and
the Son and the Holy Spirit.

HIV

The sweet one and the sour blood
went to the beach.
The sour blood, this was burnt.
The sweet blood went into the sea
and ran back healthy.

Also for treating arthritis, to much acid in the body, diabetes, gout, hangover (alcohol abuse), cancer, multiple sclerosis, rheumatism

Rheumatism, gout

Gout, like a story, the Gospel tells.
Go out from the head, go out from all body limbs,
bring to the person the health again.
In the name of the Father and
the Son and the Holy Spirit.

Inflammations of all kind

Pain, inflammation, itch – shrink
do not become hard like stone
decrease – like the death in the grave.

Itching, pain, neurodermititis, arthritis, sinusitis

Open wounds

Dry up, be quiet, you fresh wound.
Grow together meat and bone
that it becomes hard
like a stone.
In the name of the Father and the Son and the Holy Spirit.

Wounds of all kind, broken bones, acne, furuncle, bleedings, period pains

Open wounds (2)
Jesus wounds are open – without a bandage.
They do not bleed, they do not swell, they also do not hurt.

Wounds of all kind, broken bones, acne, furuncle, bleedings, period pains

Burns
Holy Lorenz lay on the bed,
the blessing God - he gave him frost
he came with his holy hand,
and blows away the fire – the cold and the hot.

Burns, frostbite, fever, too high or too low body temperature

Burns (2)
Our Lord Jesus Christ moved through the land,
fire and burns – he had in his hand.
Fire - you should not splash - go low,
Fire – you should not sweat.
In 24 hours you have to go!
In the name of the Father and the Son and the Holy Spirit.

Burns, frostbite, fever

Skin diseases
The cinder and the lichen,
they flew over the sea,
the cinder came again,
the lichen was not seen.

Neurodermititis, eczema, psoriasis, ichtyosis

Allergies
Antonius fire burns everywhere,
now also in this stable,
I talk to you, I chase you away,
go now to another place and stay.

Allergies of all kind, erysipelas of animals, vein inflammation, open legs

Insect stings
Burn – go to the sea,
go to the sand,
and does not hurt any more.

Insect stings, snake bites, nettle rash, contact with jellyfish

Back pain
Pain in the back,
melt away like snow,
become a dream
and then to foam.

Back pain of all kind, Scheuermann' disease, Bekhterev's disease, sciatica, problems with the intervertebral discs

Oedema
The moon increases,
the water decreases.

Oedema, Oedema of all kind, lymph stasis

Tumours
Tumour, catch the sun and shrinks
stop on this point,
and let you see here never again!

Tumours of all kind, cancer, myomas, cysts, ulcers

Epilepsy
You tremble like an eel,
the life becomes a torture,
the foam on your mouth leaves,
you become healthy.

Epilepsy, Parkinson disease, senile dementia, Alzheimer disease

Staunching blood
I go in Jesus garden
there stand three little flowers
one is called Parille
Jesus will
Blood stand still!

Corns
What is from heaven, this survive.
What I press, this passes.

Against worms of all kind
I order to you, worm, you are in the meat,
maybe – if there are one of you or more,
no matter, how many there are.
In the name of the Father and the Son and the Holy Spirit,
in the name of Jesus from Nazareth who was born in Bethlehem,
christened in the river Jordan, was tortured in Jerusalem,
went in the heaven from the Mount of Olives,
in fact you eat never again from the man or the woman's meat and drink never again from
the blood.
In the name of God. Amen.

Swellings (for example after a bruise)

You should not swell. You should not stream. You should be so pure, like the word of God.
In the name of the Father and the Son and the Holy Spirit.

Entanglement (indigestions of all kind,
also animals, which do not want to eat anymore)
You are caught by the water, then you get help from the father in heaven.
You are caught by the feed, then you get help from the mother in heaven.
You are caught by the wind, then you get help from child in heaven.
In the name of the Father and the Son and the Holy Spirit.

Colic
Colic – become good,
I swear to you by the holy blood,
you may not torment further up to the grave,
so true - as God has returned the life to his son. In the name of the
light.
(the hand circles the belly and is shaken during naming)

Announced three times

General sayings, which work for all diseases
Holy Atisha, you cure wounds and pain.
Bad to the hell, the good into the heart.
In the name of Light and Love. Amen

Atisha was – what I have found out already – a Buddhistic saint.

Another general saying, which works well
You - (name of the disease like shingles, tumour, MS, warts, gangrene etc.) hear my
order:
I banish you on the top of the highest mountain,
in the deepest shaft,
on the ground of the sea
and in the endless desert;
You (name of the patient) should never be tormented by (name of the
disease like shingles, tumour, MS, warts, gangrene etc.) again. In the name
of the Father and the Son and the Holy Spirit.

Mental inputs

Mental inputs work under the same principle as the "stereotyped intention" in autogenic training (AT). In AT the patients give themselves stereotyped intentions during a deep relaxation. These are mnemotechnic verses, which can prevent undesired behaviour, fears, addictions, etc. Something similar happens under hypnosis: While the clients are in a trance, the suggestions, for example to reduce weight or to stop smoking, will be given to the subconsciousness.

There are still many (unjustified) prejudices against hypnosis. Reasons are partial superstition, but also the results of the sensational press. To really use AT, it is necessary to train regularly.

Mental inputs are as effective, but a lot easier to use. If the mental behaviour should be changed, then this is the right technique. It helps to reduce fears, or compulsive acts, to change addictive behaviour, etc. In fact, this is a form of hypnosis, but without trance.

This is a good preparatory exercise: Choose a test person (the gender does not matter) of average intelligence, who is willing to participate without any reservation. The test person should sit at a table. Then you give the test person a common pendulum, which should be hold between two fingers over the tabletop. The arm should not be rested and the pendulum should be still. (Complete stillness will not be possible, because of the unwilling contraction of the muscles).

Now stand behind the test person and place your hands on top of the head. Focus on the pendulum and try to make it swing from left to right. It may take 2 or 3 minutes, but then the pendulum will start to swing, slowly at first but then very clearly.

If the pendulum is swinging very clearly, force the pendulum mentally in another direction. If it swings from left to right, then make it swing to the front and back. This will also happen after some time.

Make this experiment with different test persons. You will see, that this experiment will work with almost every person.

This experiment shows, like many others, how your own thoughts may influence another person.

Try to do this experiment with the pendulum repeatedly and with different persons. Just like you can train your muscles, you can also train your mental ability!

In the second half of the last century, the USA and the USSR performed many experiments about telepathy. The results were very positive.

Just like we can influence a pendulum, we can also influence a person.

There are several exercises, which improve your own sensitivity and also allow us to influence other people in a positive way. The "magic word" is to keep quiet. Get used to being silent for a few minutes every day. During my shamanistic training, the instructing shaman put great emphasis on "being quiet". Right at the beginning he asked us to be quiet for 5 minutes - not just acoustically, but mental. That means 5 minutes of thinking nothing. Really not thinking at all is a very difficult task. Those who meditate regularly know, what I mean. "Be quiet" does not mean to concentrate on a certain object (for example candle light) for some time, but to think about NOTHING.

Allow yourself a short break everyday and be quiet. At first, it will probably be quite difficult to be quiet for a minute, but soon you will be able to extend this time of silence.

Back to our mental inputs:

At first you have to work out the wording and, if possible, together with the client. These wordings, which you want to give into the client have to be formulated individually for the client's problems. This is the most important rule: the wordings have to be short, concisely, and positive. Positive means: No negations, because the subconsciousness does not know negations! If the client suffers, for example from fears, then the wording: "You have no fear!" does not help at all, because the subconsciousness does not know negations and just understands: "You have fear!" And this causes the complete opposite of what we actually wanted! The wording: "You are always brave and manage every problem!" is much better. Instead of: "You do not smoke and you hate cigarettes" choose the sentence: "Smoking does not matter and you love fresh air." After each sentence, you can put this sentence: "You feel better every day and in every regard." The client should say this sentence every day multiple times aloud or quietly. Émile Coué (1857-1927), the founder of the modern "Autosuggestion", was very successful in healing with the help of this sentence.

You do not have to speak the wordings aloud. Thinking is sufficient. But concentrate on these wordings and avoid digressing! Everything what you are thinking about, also goes to the subconsciousness of your client. That means, you really have to be convinced of this method. If you think: "I wonder if that works", then these thoughts will get to the subconsciousness of your client and cause doubts. In this case, failure will be the result!

Work on some wordings for the most common mental problems, like claustrophobia, fear of narrow rooms, fear of storm, etc.

This is the most effective way of a treatment:
Sit yourself at the side of your client and place one hand on the back of the head and the other on the forehead. Calm down and synchronise your breathing and the breathing of your client: If the client breathes in, you also breathe in and when the client breathes out, you breathe out as well!

It will take some time, until both will be breathing in the same rhythm. If it works, then you can begin to give your client the wordings: Every time you breathe out, you think your wordings. For example:

Breathe in, and then during breathing out: "You are always brave and manage every problem!"

Breathe in, and then during breathing out: "You feel better every day and in every regard!"

Mental inputs have to be short to fit in one breath of air. When they are longer, divide them in that way:

Breathe in, and then during breathing out: 1st part of the wording.
Breathe in, and then during breathing out: 2nd part of the wording.

The treatment should at least take 5 minutes, but it can also take 10 minutes or longer to give your client the wordings. Remember to have a clock nearby to control the time.

Your hands should really rest on the forehead and on the back of the head. I made experiments placing the hands on the sides (just above the ears) or on the shoulders. But the results were much better, when the hands are placed on the forehead and on the back of the head.

Of course you can treat every disease this way and not just mental problems. It is also possible to combine - with this variation I achieved the best results:

Treat a disease of the body with hands-on healing and give then the mental input: "You feel better every day and in every regard!"

If the client repeats this wording multiple times a day aloud or in silence, then success is practically guaranteed!

Pelvic Obliquity

The purpose of the skeleton is to hold the body against gravity. This can only be managed, if it is upright in square, and the spine is able to swing symmetrical around the plumb during walking. If this is not the case, every joint - from head to toe - can block, which leads to increased wear marks in the joints and also to dysfunctions outside the locomotors system, due to the disturbed spinal nerves and the nerves of the autonomic nervous system (sympathetic nervous system, parasympathetic nervous system).

The reason for the structure defect is usually the so called "leg length inequality", which causes or intensifies the symptoms or the pains like sciatica, lumbago, shoulder-arm-syndrome, headaches, cervical-spine-, thoracic-spine-, lumbar-spine-syndrome, blood flow disorders, problems with the spinal discs and spinal disc herniation, vision disorders, tinnitus, migraine, degeneration of the bones, cramped and uptight back muscles, scoliosis, furry fingers, numb fingers and arms, sliding vertebra, tennis elbow, hollow back, crooked teeth, groins pain, lymph congestion, bone and muscular atrophy, concentration disorders, thyroid disorder, myocardial insufficiency and cardiac arrhythmia, nerve diseases in general, renal dysfunction, sensibility disorder, numbness, dysfunction of the hypophysis, etc.

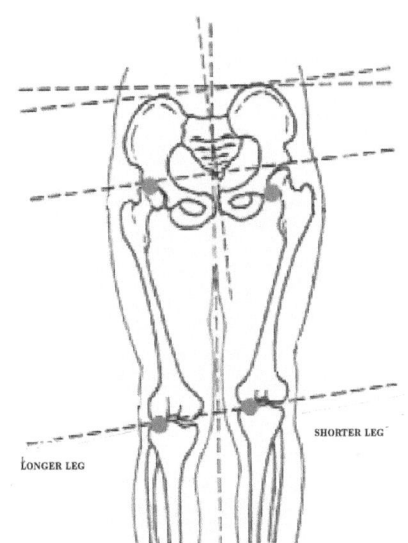

Usually the false posture is compensated with one leg, which leads to 3 basic posture types, but most common are the hybrid forms:

– Pelvic inclination towards the shorter leg: pelvic obliquity
– Knock knees on the side of the longer leg
– Drop foot on the side of the shorter leg

It is remarkable, that a lot of the leg length inequalities und pelvic obliquities are caused by a false position of one or both leg joints and can be corrected without problems.

In my opinion the correction of the pelvic obliquity is the biggest and most important help for the human being to obtain or to restore health! That is why the checking of the leg length is usually the first step, when a patient comes to see me.

Many operations can be avoided and cancelled that way.

What are the reasons for a pelvic obliquity?

The human body and especially the spine are since the "invention" of the erect posture quite sensitive. Sitting a lot, and often with crossed legs, causes the dislocation of the hip joints from the acetabulum, which looks like leg length inequalities. Fact is, that usually the legs have the same length and the difference is just caused through the false position of the joints.

The manual correction (only natural health professionals or physiotherapists are allowed to perform this - or only on relatives and friends):

Usually I teach the manual correction in personal practice. Always remember to ask the patient, if he suffers from osteoporosis or if he has an artificial hip joint, before you begin the manual correction. In both cases, you have to skip the treatment, because you could damage a lot more, than you could help.

This is a description of the manual correction and how you can check the difference in leg length, before and after the correction on the spiritual way:

The patient is lying on the couch or on the floor. You stand at the foot and then you raise carefully both feet, until the legs are at a degree of at least 45°.

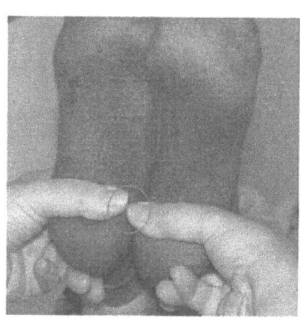 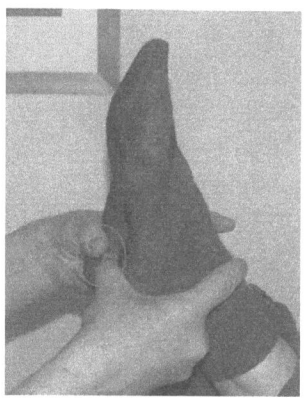

The different leg length can be seen at the soles of the feet. When there is no difference, both heels should be on the same level. Unfortunately, this is rarely the case. I have already seen differences over 5 cm.

If you lay your thumbs on the heels, then you can detect the difference very clearly. Look at your thumbnails and you can see the exact difference.

Then the leg, which is "too long", will be raised like this: The thigh should be raised at a

90° angle to the lying patient. The lower leg is raised in the air.

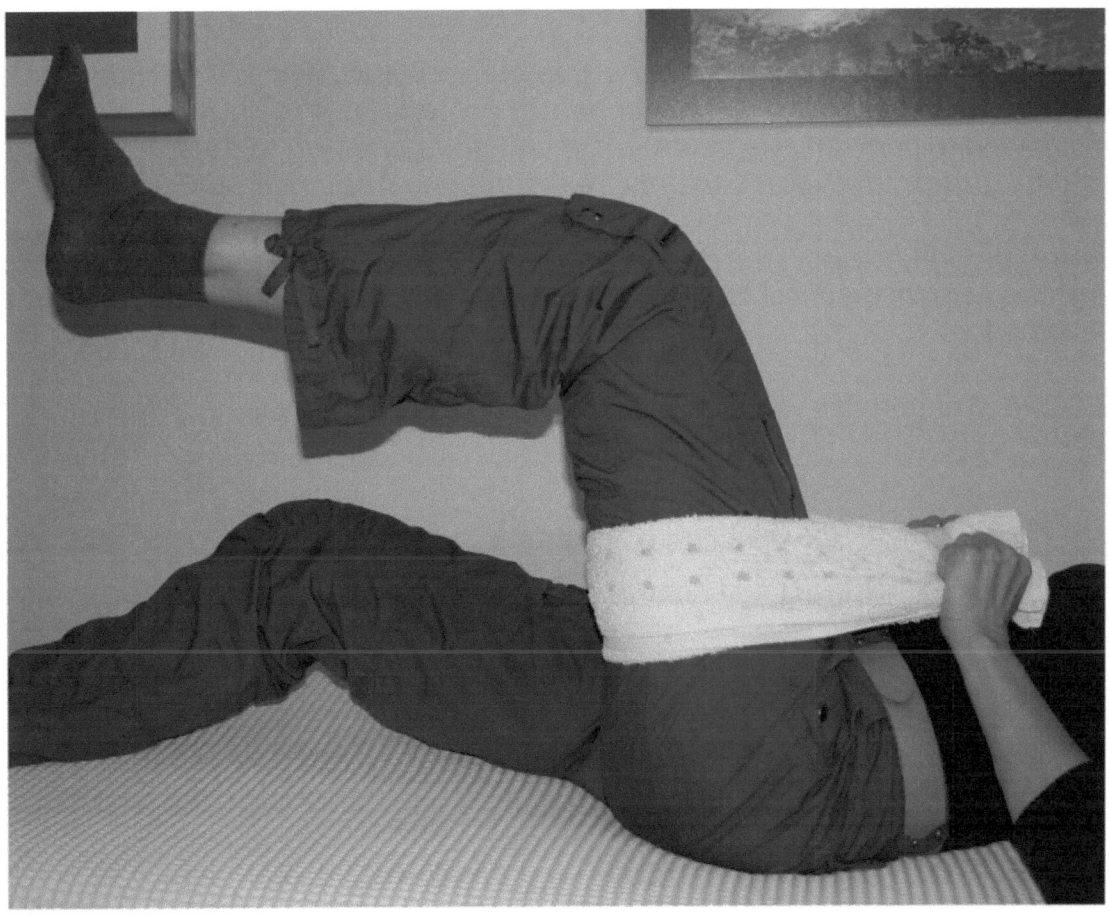

Then you take a towel or the patient's hand to draw the joint of the thigh to the body. The leg has to be limber during this exercise.

While the patient is drawing the joint into the acetabulum, you carefully press the leg lightly at the knee downwards. (It does not work, when the leg is tensed! Therefore: All muscles have to be limber.) While doing this, you will hear a soft "creak", when the joint is back in the acetabulum again.

Now you should check the leg length again. In some cases, you have to repeat this treatment. It is also possible, that the other leg now seems longer than the one, which was just treated. In that case, both joints slid out of their acetabulum.

Do not forget to tell the patient, that during the next days the muscles in the legs and the hip can hurt, like when you have sore muscles. That happens because the muscles - after many years of false position - have to get used to their correct position again.

The patient can do this correction on his own several times a week. The best time is before falling asleep. That way the joint will stay correctly in the acetabulum!

It is important to do this before falling asleep. If you usually read in bed, go to the toilet, and then fall asleep, you should perform this exercise after the toilet and right before falling asleep.

Important: This treatment does not belong to the activities, which a spiritual healer is allowed to do. Only doctors, natural health professionals, physiotherapists, etc. are allowed to perform this treatment. If you do not belong to these professional groups, then you can only treat someone from your family.

It is allowed though, to show the patient or client this way of self treatment. That way they can help themselves to avoid reoccurring problems with their spine and a pelvic inclination.

THEREFORE: Treatment – no. Demonstrating for self help – yes.

The mental Erection and Straightening

Energetic help for the mental erection of the spine, possibly with straightening of the spine

The mental erection affects many levels and may, among other things, loosen karmic blockades and patterns, which have attached to the spine. The results are lesser leg length differences and lesser shoulder problems. Finally, the whole human being will be "straight".

The cells will get a new information impulse, which activates the self-regulating forces sustainably.

The loosening of blockades also enables the cleaning and reorientation of the different aura layers.

Treatment

Remember, that you are not allowed to diagnose, unless you are a doctor or a natural health professional. Therefore you are actually allowed to perform the just described way to control the leg length, but you are not allowed to tell your client, that the left or the right leg is longer. If you do, then this is a diagnosis.

It is important to remember, that you are working with God's energy, which is totally pure. This energy is the only reason for the results. You are just the transmitter and the channel for the energy.

This is what you should do: For your own information (and not as a diagnosis for your client!) you can check, if there is a pelvic obliquity or - while standing - if the shoulder blades are on the same level.

The client should stand upright. Then you check at the back the peaks of the shoulder blades. The arms should hang to the sides. Maybe someone could take a photo, while you point with your fingers to the height of the peaks of the shoulder blades.

You can also use the method, which is already described. Then you can control the success of the light energy as well. You can check the leg length, if the client lays on his back and the legs are raised at an angle of 45°.

Hold the heels next to each other and look, if the heels are on the same level. If they are not at the same level, then you may mark the difference with lines to check the success easier. In some cases (especially if the difference is very obvious) the success is not visible at once. But the client will feel the working energy during the next days.

Traditionally the client should lie on his belly, but it also works lying on the back, sitting down, or from the distance. At first you centre yourself, as usual when doing energy work, and you ask for contact to the straightening energy and for the allowance to straighten your client energetically.

The energy you ask for, is Christ's energy, pure love energy, real straightening energy. Then you form a circle with your hands. It can be done with only one hand as well (put the tip of your thumb and the tip of your index together so they will form an O). Imagine a ray of light coming from heaven right through this circle. This ray of light will be guided between the shoulder blades, which means you put your hands between the shoulder blades of your client to bring the light in his body. Then you move your hands to bring the energy lower to the lumbar spine.

Those who like it less difficult, can visualise a ray of light entering through the crown chakra going through the heart into the hand chakras. You lay your hands on the client's spine (like in a reiki treatment) and let them rest there for about 3 minutes. After 3 minutes you move your hand a hand's width lower and you let the energy flow there for another 3 minutes. The whole treatment of the spine in this way takes about 20-30 minutes.

Then the straightening is finished. Sometimes - depending on the client's condition - the straightening can be repeated after a week.

Now you can check, if the legs have the same length and if the shoulder blades are on the same level.

After that a reiki or a healing treatment will do well, but it is not necessary.

Another variant is, to send the straightening energy mentally to the client, beginning from the cervical spine and then vertebra after vertebra down to the tail bone and back up again.

You can do this treatment also as a distant treatment. Arrange a certain appointment and do this treatment in your imagination, while you concentrate on the image of your client.

To treat yourself, ask your higher self, if you are allowed to give yourself this treatment in about 20 minutes. Then you do this treatment in your imagination. After 20 minutes you lay down and you receive the energy.

Spine and the according Vertebras

C1 – C7 = cervical spine

1:Blood supply, head, brain, ears, sympathetic nervous system

2:Eyes, sinuses, hearing nerves, tongue, forehead

3:Cheeks, facial bones, teeth, facial nerve

4:Nose, mouth, lips

5:Vocal cord, throat

6:Neck muscles, shoulders, tonsils

7:Thyroid, shoulders, elbows

Th1 – Th12: Thoracic spine

T1:Arms, wrists, finger, gullet und windpipe

T2:Heart, coronary vessels

T3:Lung, bronchia, thorax, breasts

T4:Gall, gall bladder

T5:Liver, solar plexus, general blood supply

T6:Stomach

T7:Pancreas, duodenum

T8:Spleen

T9:Adrenal glands

T10:Kidneys

Th11:Urethra

Th12:Small intestine, lymph system

L1 – L5: Lumbar spine

1:Colon, groin

2:Appendix, belly, thigh

3:Genitals, uterus, bladder, knee

4:Prostate, lower back, sciatica

5:Lower leg, ankles, feet

Os sacrum / sacral bone: hip bones, bottom

Coccyx / tail bone: rectum, anus

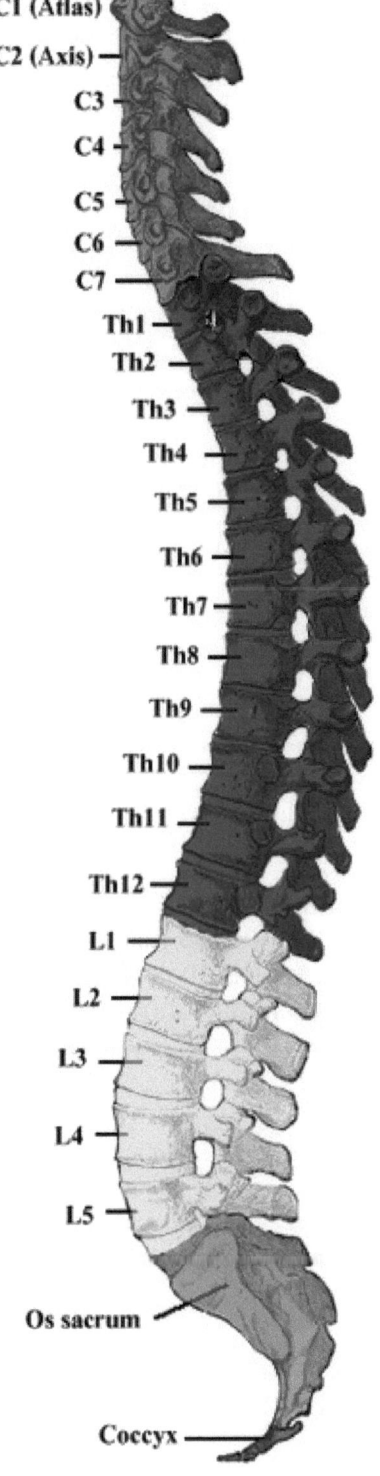

Lumbago / Herniated Disc

The herniated disc can happen at every vertebra, when a part of the disc leaves its correct position, which squeezes the nerve. This herniation can be cured with immobilisation and warmth.

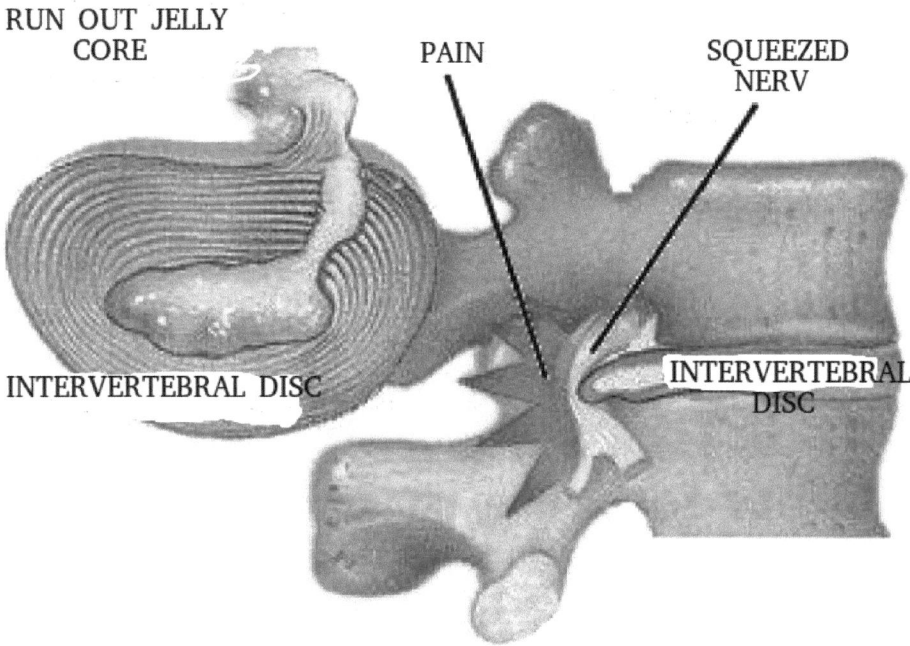

If this happens often, then the discs can be damaged forever and the pulpous nucleus can leak out, which leaves just the empty covering of the disc. In this case, and if you have a good orthopaedist, an artificial disc can be implanted. Some patients have no problems, but others are constantly under pain because the nerve is permanently irritated.

Inform yourself in every detail about the risks of an operation. Artificial discs are not yet used for a long time.

Part III

Legal Suggestions

Spiritual Healing is completely legally in many countries. Please, find out about how the law situation is in your country. You get more information about it in your city hall or the city administration.

For example - Since early 2004 spiritual healing is legal in Germany - if you take care of certain requirements!

A healer must not make a diagnosis and he is only allowed to "activate the vital energy in his patients". This means, you are allowed to treat diseases, if you activate the self-regulating forces, but you must not make a diagnosis in any kind and you are also not allowed to give or prescribe medicine. If you discover interfering fields or you get information about an undiscovered disease, then you may treat these problems, but you are not allowed to tell the patient about what you just found out, about for example the bile or the heart. You can give general hints though, like: "Maybe you should check up your bile, because I read in a magazine, that the bile may play a role in your kind of problems. Do that just for safety reasons." Maybe the "orthodox medical practitioner" will find something, what can be treated in a conventional way. If not, maybe you have gotten a wrong information. It is also possible, that the disease cannot be diagnosed yet, because it is too early. Some diseases (for example cancer) develop over several years from the early stage of a degenerative cell to a detectable tumour. Another example is a savourer (lots of alcohol, fat food, etc.), whose liver is already disturbed, but does not yet cause problems. Even if nothing is diagnosed, you should treat the body part, where you found something "strange" more intensive. If there is still no diagnosed tumour after five years, then your treatment may be the reason or the "academic medicine" was successful. Whatever it was, does not really matter: The main thing is, that the patient is healthy again. It is unimportant, who performed this "miracle". The patient is feeling better. This is important. This is the main task of spiritual healing and this always has to be your first priority.

Do not forget to tell your patients, that your treatment is no substitute for a medical attendance or a diagnosis. You can hang up a posting in your treatment room, but "what you have in black and white, you can carry home". In other words: Let your patients sign a form. Then your patients cannot claim later, that they cannot remember this statement.

The best way is to give each patient a form with the statement, which they should sign. Do this prior to the first treatment!

This should be the content:

Spiritual healing activates the self regulating forces and is no substitute for the diagnosis or the treatment of a doctor or a natural health professional. With my signature I confirm to have received this statement prior to the treatment.

Place, date,
Signature of the patient
(if you are under age, signature of the parents)

This text was worked out by the legal advisor of the umbrella organisation of spiritual healing and should be "ironclad" as he is a lawyer and a notary.

However you must not let the patients sign the forms, tell them that this is just a formality and then make empty promises, prescribe medicine and do other illegal tasks, like for example promise cure. Again: Nobody can promise a cure, neither a doctor nor a natural health professional...and also no healer.

Always remember: Your treatment may be successful. Perhaps a paralytic will leave his wheelchair and is able to walk again. But those spontaneous recoveries are the exception! Usually the work of a healer is a lengthy piece of work and sometimes it takes 2-3 weeks of sessions to show first results.

Distant treatments are a difficult theme – not regarding the performance, but the legal aspect! If you think, you can just start your treatments after stating that this is not a substitute for a medical attendance, then you are wrong. ***That does not apply to distant treatments!*** Distant treatments for money are not allowed in principle. A doctor or a natural health professional is not allowed to do that either and healers cannot be situated juristically better than these professions. (Furthermore in my opinion the patient should always know his healer personally.) If you ignore this prohibition, you will get some adhortatory letters quickly. If you ask for a "donation" after the treatment, you could easily come into conflict with the law. And if you offer distant treatments for free and you deny payment, then a lot of patients will assume a snag. If the treatment was successful, you can ask the patient to donate something to a charity organisation of his own choice (the patient should chose the amount).

Money is a very sensitive theme. The more you want it, the more it dissipates. But if you accept it as a necessary form of energy, which - after you spent it as a distant treatment and in form of the resulting donations of your patients - comes back to you, then you will recognise, that even distant treatments will bring in something. That sounds complicated, but it is not. It is just an exchange of energy: You give a distant treatment, the patient gives a donation and somebody else will give something back to you again.

Financial Tips

"Money" is a difficult theme for several people. The DGH e.V. (German Association) recommends for a treatment a maximum of 80,00 Euro per hour. If the treatment lasts 15 minutes and we add a welcome, a conversation and saying goodbye, then it will take about 30 minutes which will cost 40,00 Euro. Even if the 1st consultation takes longer, then you will still be at the upper end of the price scale, when you get 40,00 Euro. I do not think, that this is inappropriate but it is still "well-paid". Remember, that most of the sick people already suffer for a long time (a healer is always the last hope and will not be visited until all other therapies have failed). Some patients may have lost their jobs, because of the disease or just have a small pension, due to their inability to work.

Your treatment is certainly worth a lot – but some just cannot pay the price. Nevertheless: Never refuse to treat someone just because he cannot pay you. Whatever you give, will come back to you sometime. This concerns benefits, but also rejections towards your patients.

Think about putting up a "donation plate" in form of a money box. Then everybody can give as much as he can.

If you work part-time as a healer and you have a job, which assures your livelihood, then of course you can treat your patients for free. I did that for a long time, until I decided to give up my job and focus on healing and teaching.

Code of Conduct and basic rules for your behaviour towards persons seeking help

These texts are from the German Association for Spiritual Healing DGH e.V. (in big letters), followed by my opinions (in smaller blue letters).

I. 1.The client's freedom of the will remains unaffected. In particular, I do not leverage to start or to continue to come to my sessions.

The client is responsible and decides freely, if he wants to stop or to continue the treatment of spiritual healing. Clients must not be cheated, be manipulated, or be influenced subtly, like for example with the help of showing or giving letters of appreciation, magazine articles, etc. without request. The healer is not allowed to commit the client to a prior defined number of sessions. This rule should avoid the development of a dependency.

My opinion: Of course every client has the right to decide, how to be treated. It is his own choice to go to a doctor, a natural health professional, or to a healer. A lot of times the patients, who come to a healer for help and advice are "beyond treatment". Many of them have already been to a lot of doctors, and visiting a healer is like catching at a straw. Some healers (especially when several healings were successful) tend to speak badly about the traditional medicine or about other types of therapy. But every type of therapy has its eligibility though. Therefore we, as healers, should refrain from trying to influence the persons seeking help in any kind. Letters of appreciation, which are presented without request, badmouthing of certain types of therapies, etc. have to be avoided.

If a person seeking help asks, if you have already successful treated, for example neurodermititis, migraine, etc. then of course you can tell him, that you already have done this. You should mention this in a factual and neutral way though. Quite common is the question about how many sessions are needed to cure asthma, cardiac arrhythmias, or something like that. Be careful, that your answer does not imply a fixed number of sessions. This would lead to a dependency, which has to be avoided by all means.

2. I am aware of my responsibility towards my client in everything I say, write, do or refrain from.

My opinion: As a healer, we take over a part of the responsibility of the client's health. Many clients view us similar to a doctor. But if the healer is not a doctor as well, then he is not allowed to influence the medical therapy. This is a common question: "I feel a lot better. May I stop taking the physician-directed medicine?" Only the doctor can answer this question. Therefore send your client to the doctor, who prescribed the medicine. It is his task to examine the patient and to decide, if there really has been a recovery. If this is the case, then the doctor (and only the doctor) will adapt the medication. Remember that there is medicine, which has to be discontinued slowly to avoid health problems. Only the doctor can make this decision.

3.Never promise healing or even just relief.

Obeying this rule protects the healer, especially from legal consequences resulting from the laws in Germany, Austria and in most of the Swiss cantons. On top of this the client should not be lead to a dependency, due to promises of success or statements, which could be interpreted in that way.

My opinion: No doctor or natural health professional is allowed to promise a successful treatment. This applies also to healers. Of course the healer may (and should) arouse optimism in the patient to overcome the disease. But that is all.

4. I do not present myself as a "faith healer".

The term "faith healer" causes hope for an instant, total healing for everybody.

My opinion: Some healers may experience "miracles". But these are the exception and unfortunately not the rule. You can read about "faith healers" or "miracle doctors" in magazines, which sometimes raises the circulation of the magazines "wonderfully". But as a healer, you should not ever use the term "wonder". That would only cause false hopes in the clients.
During the last 120 years, millions of sick people went to Lourdes in France in search of healing. Around 7000 were cured, but only 66 of them are approved as "miracle". But that's enough of the "wonder" theme.

5. I advise my clients to not build their hopes just on me.

The client should be encouraged to trust in his self-regulating forces. The healer is just a companion on the way of the client and should express that towards the client very clearly. His tasks should not be presented as a substitute for medical or natural health treatments.

My opinion: A healer can never be a substitute for a medical treatment. In an ideal situation, he could be an addition. Always explain your clients, that this is not an "either or" but an "as well as". Even if the client is coming for a treatment regularly, he should also see his doctor regularly as well. That way any subjectively felt improvement can be controlled objectively.

6. The centre of my work is the commitment to encounter clients patiently, sensitively, and compassionately.

This decree is for healers a matter of course. There are limits of what is reasonable though. Nobody can demand from a healer to be at disposal regardless of his time and power (for example accepting phone calls at 2 at night).

My opinion: The clients, who go to a healer search for something, what they cannot get from a doctor. Our health system cannot afford a heart-to-heart talk and a personal care at the doctor's office; therefore we should offer the client time and compassion. But we also have to make clear, that we are not available 24 hours on 7 days a week. Healers also have and need a private life to get fit again for the clients on the next day. Fixed office hours should be considered, no matter, if it is a healer or a doctor. A separate phone number with mail box (ISDN-connection) helps to avoid disturbances of family life through phone calls in the evening or on weekends.

7. I explain my clients, that it is my task to activate their self-regulating forces, which is not a substitute to the treatment of a doctor or a natural health professional. This could be with the help of a very well visible posting, or the patients get a form before the treatment, which they have to sign. The client has to be informed about the expected procedures of the sessions, their duration, and also the price at the first contact, or at the first meeting at the latest.

Answer any questions directly and without excuses. The client has to be informed prior to unpredicted changes of the procedure of the session and the client may decide freely, if to accept or to refuse. It is recommended, that healer and client talk about the DGH-sheet "Information" in detail to remove possible ambiguity. After that, healer and client should both sign this sheet. Point 2 of this rule does not apply to group intercessions and similar sessions.

My opinion: Legally the posting in the treatment room of the healer is enough to remind the patients, that a healer only activates the self-regulating forces, which is no substitute to a medical therapy. But "what you have in black and white will also be accepted in front of a judge or the health office". In other words: If there are court proceedings, then a signed statement helps to proof, that you informed your client sufficiently. Then the client (or the surviving dependants) cannot claim, that he did not know about the statement.

II. Guidelines for fees

1. My willingness to help is not related to the solvency of my clients.

The healer's willingness to help should not depend on the financial solvency of the client. Healers cannot be generally asked to work only for free – especially, if they are working full-time and rely on revenues. The fees should be transparent and attention to socially weak clients is essential.

My opinion: Especially reiki practitioner work with the energy exchange. Although the prices for the seminars are quite high (which they may be, as the preparation of a seminar takes a lot of time and the actual lessons are not done in 1 or 2 hours either), this does not imply, that the treatments have to expensive as well.

Always remember, that most of the clients suffer for a long time and many of them – because of their disease – already had heavy losses. Clearly your treatment is worth a lot. But not everybody can pay much. I decided to put up a "donation box", in which everybody, who cannot pay my usually fees (at the moment 30 Euro for a half hour treatment), can put whatever he can afford. Those who have to live on benefit (and believe me: you cannot live on that), can return the favour with a prayer.

2. I attend to the guidelines for fees recommended by the DGH e.V.

Generally, only the time of the session should be charged. The maximum should be € 80,-/sfr 130,- per 60 minutes. Voluntary gifts or donations do not apply to the constraints under no. II. 1-4. This guideline applies to phone sessions as well.

My opinion: Those who have the habit to meditate several times a day or prior to each healing session (not just a few healers do this), are not allowed to charge this time to the client's account, even if this meditation might be necessary for the healer.

3. I only charge tasks which were done in the presence of the client.

You cannot charge: distant healing, intercession in absence of the person seeking help. Both are services the client cannot control for sure in their number und duration. Therefore this applies not for sessions on the phone. If a client missed an appointed session, then you are not allowed to charge him.

My opinion: Basically, distant treatments also should not be charged. Doctors and natural health professionals are not allowed to perform distant treatments. Healers are also not allowed to perform distant treatments for money, because that would violate the competition law. I already mentioned that in this script.

I never demand advance payment.

Cashless payments, like for example cheque, or credit card, are also an advance payment.

III. My relationship to approved healing professions

1. I look after a good relationship and cooperation to everybody involved in professional healing.

The healer should not defame doctors and other healing professions. As far as possible, the healer should seek exchange with representatives of other healing professions.

2. I will not diagnose, examine, give therapy, or perform healing arts in a legally defined way. Medicine (also Bach flowers, teas, etc.) will neither be recommended nor prescribed or given. I point out, that the medical attendance still should be done by the doctor/natural health professional; which means, I also do not advise against: doctor's visit, intake of medication, therapies, or operations.

The healer should not create the impression, that he can detect diseases reliably and precisely. Many healers do get intuitive impressions about kind and cause of problems though (for example through seeing and feeling the aura). Therefore you should give hints just in form of general questions (for example "Have you been to a doctor?"). Healers also should not create the impression, that they cure certain diseases. Healers do not treat diseases – they treat sick people. Doing this, they do not eliminate certain symptoms or underlying physical injuries, but they support the client to activate their self-regulating forces.

According to the German legislature the performance of "healing arts" is "every task performed professionally or commercially to diagnose, heal, or ease diseases, sufferings, or physical injuries on human beings, even though when performed in service of others" (Non-Medical Practitioners Act § 1 (2)). (According to the interpretation of the courts it suffices, if the client gets such an impression.)

In Austria every "task, which is reserved to the doctors, performed commercially on a larger amount of people" is prosecutable, if performed "without the education, which is necessary to become a doctor" (§ 184 of the Austrian criminal code); according to the Act on the Medical Profession and other supplementary laws these tasks are the examination, diagnosis, and treatment of patients. A similar legal concept you can find in those Swiss cantons, which allow the performance of healing arts only to "medicine persons".

3. I do not use misleading titles and job designations.

The client must not get the impression, that the healer represents something, which he is not. This wrong impression can cause, for example the wearing of typical work clothing (white gown), and holding a bought title, or an academic title without permission. Basically I respect every colleague, who works according to these guidelines on another base of conviction than me.

IV. Tolerance

No healer is allowed to vilify or to defame another healer, due to ideology. This does not concern the right to freedom of opinion; personal convictions <u>should</u> be expressed in a factual matter though, without personal offence.

V. Promotion

Every promotion should show restraint and should primarily be information for the clients.

Promotion should not contain for example: promises of success; defaming other methods, colleagues or representatives of other healing professions; references to letter of thanks, awards and specialisation on certain diseases; other misleading statements.

VI. Confidentiality

All personal information, the client entrusts me with, I treat strictly confidential.

A transfer in anonymous form (which means without giving personal data) is allowed - for example as part of information exchange with colleagues or representatives of other healing professions.

VII. Duty of Disclosure

As part of the obligation to secrecy I am willing to bare every detail about my actions towards the DGH e.V. *This rule is necessary to check the observance of the code, if required.*

VIII. Supporting the Ethic-Commission

If I become acquainted to offences against the principles of this code of conduct, I will point it out to the concerning healer in an adequate form. In this cases, I can also ask the "ethic-commission" for help and/or support.

This code including the explanations was decided by the board of directors of the DGH e.V. on 24.9.1995 and <u>changed on 14.2.1998 and on 8.5.2004.</u> The content should be discussed and if necessary modified in regular periods.

Tips for your own office and your own website

Again and again I am asked the same questions: How do I open up an office for treatments, what do I have to do, register a business, taxes etc. These are the most common questions and answers:

After an education or an initiation of a healing system (no matter if usui-reiki, baraka, shamballa-reiki or others) many people sooner or later have the wish to treat other human beings.

Quite often you can hear or read, that a real healer should not promote his work, because "every sick person will find the appropriate healer". Interesting theory - unfortunately that is only partly right. Those who have a large circle of friends, go to parties a lot, or cultivate contacts in other ways, will maybe also be lucky to get patients that way, and just use word-of-mouth advertising. In reality most healers are rather quiet and introverted persons. Which patient should find them?

Imagine either being a patient who has just gotten a terrible diagnosis from his doctor: "You have cancer or asthma, diabetes, neurodermititis etc.", or a patient who already suffers for years from a chronic disease, which cannot be cured by traditional medicine. How should such a person find a healer? Certainly not in the phone book.

When I decided to work as a healer full-time, I advertised in local magazines, which are distributed for free. For example: "Helping with spiritual healing, hands-on healing, conjuring of warts and shingles. Phone..." It is important to advertise constantly, because the future patients do not remember your phone number to call you sometime. When they become sick and need help, then they will look in the magazines, thinking: "There used to be an advertisement". You can also advertise in local weekly magazines or in common local or nationwide esoteric magazines. Look around the magazines in a shop and ask about the prices to run an advertisement. Another possibility is a free listing in the address list of the spiritual healers.

What do you need for your own office? First of all, a desk with a useful appointment calendar (your brain might be reliable, but some day there will be too many appointments and you forget them). I did not keep patient files for a long time. But as I repeatedly confused Mrs. X and her stomach problems, with Mrs. Y and her neurodermititis, I realized that I need a desk, an appointment calendar and useful files. You can get cheap file cards in A5 (half a sheet of writing paper) in every paper and office shop. A card box in the same size is not expensive either and keeps everything in order, which is important.

Many healers use a couch. A real treatment couch, like used by masseurs, is not cheap, but an investment for life. If you like it less expensive: Just use a bed or an upholstered couch found often in guest rooms.

Before you start your treatments you have to register a business. In Germany you have to do this for every independent activity, which brings in money. You can register at the local authority (if you are unsure, ask at the town hall). When healing was still illegal, many registered as health consultants or life consultants. Today it is not a problem to register as "spiritual healer", or similar. It is recommended though, to print out and take with you the verdict and the file reference of the Federal Constitutional Court (on the website of the DGH e.V.), just to be on the safe side. The local authority reports the registration of a business to the appropriate finance authority, which will send you a form, which is a disclosure of information. You have to fill in, how much you think, you will probably earn per year. Careful: If you estimate too generously, you might have to pay value added tax in advance. Those who earn 17.000 Euro or more per year (this is an example for germany and some other european countries) - (I think that used to be the limit, but ask your finance authority for details), have to pay value added tax. If you earn less than that, then you are a "small businessman" and you do not have to transfer the value added tax (and you will not have to do all the paperwork either)! Additionally, you will be registered automatically at the chamber of commerce. All self-employed persons become members automatically. The membership is free, if you earn less than 5200 Euro per year. If you earn more, it is not expensive either. Last but not least, you might hear from the occupational insurance association. They will pay (rather unwillingly though), if you have an accident during work. The dues are not that high, but still annoying, because there is no real service in return, in my opinion.

Do not forget the subscription for health insurance and pension insurance. As a self-employed person you can (yet) decide, how to be insured. With a small income and if there are family members, who should also be insured, the statutory health insurance might be the best choice. If you are alone, then the private health insurance could be better. Nobody knows, if you will ever get enough of the statutory pension insurance to enjoy a carefree rest of your life. A private pension insurance offers probably a lot more benefits. But everyone has to decide that on his own. My Tip: Those who have a demand for disability and invalidity pension, should stay voluntarily in that insurance paying the minimum contribution, and conclude an additional private pension.

As the time of the treatment can be long, healers should think about playing music in the background. For example some CD's (available at Amazon or in a bookshop). Of course, you also need a CD-player and an amplifier. A combination of both is a good choice as well. Careful: Those who have registered a business and do the healing treatments in their own office (even though if it is just a work room in your own house), have to pay for the licence of the music. If you have a radio in the "office premises" or just at the reception, then you have to pay radio licence fees (for example in germany and some other european countries).

If you use your car on business to do home visits (you can offset expenses against tax), then you also have to pay radio licence fees for your car radio. By the way, you do not have to pay licence for import-CDs. Just look at the CD. If there is a GEMA label, then you also have to pay GEMA fees. In Germany and some european countries.

If you do not know, what GEMA actually is: GEMA collects the money for the musicians and composers, who created the music. It is like going to a concert and paying for a ticket. Those who do not have registered a business (which means: who work for free), do not have to pay GEMA fees either, because a private use of the CD is already included in the purchase price. This also applies to those, who treat people in their private rooms for free. In this case, the music is "private enjoyment", because you are allowed to play your (legally purchased) CDs to your guests in your own home for free. All those regulations are quite complicated. Therefore, you better take a look at the GEMA website www.gema.de or you call them and ask.

Besides, the main principle for a treatment should be silence and serenity. The patients already experienced a hectic atmosphere at the doctor or in the hospital. Many successful healings are caused by the healer talking to the patient, listening to him, and giving him time. Healing is always also working with the soul of the patient, and it does not matter, if the patient has diabetes or asthma, cardiac arrhythmias, or neurodermititis, or something else. Even though our work is different to the "traditional medicine", you should understand the common terminology. Some doctors tell the patients, that they need to do a "lumbar puncture", but do not mention, that it will be quite painful to put a needle into the spinal cord, to draw "nerve water" (medically "liquor"), which will be checked for germs or symptoms for a disease. Or they tell them about a MRT examination, which is painless, but nobody tells the patients, that this means they have to lay completely motionless in a very narrow tube for about 20-30 minutes. Those who suffer from claustrophobia (fear of narrow rooms), go through absolute hell during this examination, etc.

Back to the finances: How much can you charge? Those who work part-time may set up a "donation plate". But many healers decided to work full-time, to provide all of their time for suffering people. These healers have to pay their rent, electricity, heating, etc. The baker will not give us bread rolls for free and the petrol station, where we fill our car up to go to house visits, will not give us petrol for nothing either. Therefore we have to realise, that we need to charge money for our tasks. The DGH e.V. (Dachverband Geistiges Heilen e.V. - do not confuse with the DGH = „Deutsche Gesellschaft für Hypnose") - recommends a maximum of 80,00 Euro per hour of treatment. If your treatments are shorter, then you should also charge less. Remember: Many people, who suffer from chronic diseases, are already sick for a long time. Because of their illness, they have no income anymore and live on benefit. If you charge these people 80,00 Euro per hour treatment each week, they have to pay 320,00 Euro per month. No one who lives on benefit, can raise that amount!

What you give away, that will come back to you on another way. Think about charging "these" people a social rate of 10 Euro per treatment, which applies to children and to people without income.

All my love and my best wishes to you!

God bless you!

Stefan J. Schill